Genre Realist

MW01048154

Essential Ques

What kinds of challenges transform people?

THINK HARD, THINK FAST

by Melanie Drewery
illustrated by Dan Sherbo

Chapter 1 | A Day in the Park

"Are you ready yet, Jason?" Jason's mom asked. Jason had been working on his sketch, and his room still looked like a disaster. He was supposed to go to the park with his mom and little sister, Kelly, but he still had not finished his chores.

"Almost finished!" he shouted. He shoved games, books, and shoes under his bed. He stuffed his sketch into a drawer. Now he just needed to put his laundry in the washing machine.

Kelly marched into his room. "Are you ready, are you ready," she sang. Jason shouted, "Don't nag, you pest!"

He ran to the laundry room and saw Mom there.

She sighed and said, "We have to nag, or you don't do the chores, Jason. When is Tom coming?"

Jason

laundry

Jason groaned. He'd been busy with soccer practice and homework and had forgotten to call Tom last night. "I'll call him now," he said.

Mom said, "No, it's too late. You shouldn't forget about things like this, Jason. You need to be more responsible."

"That's not fair," Jason protested.

"I've packed the picnic, and we are leaving in exactly ten minutes," Mom said. Jason knew there was no point in arguing. His mom would not change her mind.

On the walk to the park, Kelly was reading her book aloud over and over again. Mom didn't seem to notice that she was being repetitive.

"You're a fantastic reader, Kelly," Mom said.

"I'm a great reader because I can read and walk at the same time," Kelly said.

Jason was frustrated that Tom wasn't with him. Instead he had to listen to Kelly chattering away all day.

He kicked at stones as he walked behind Kelly and his mom. Suddenly Kelly skewed sideways. Her foot slipped off the curb, and her knee hit the sidewalk. "Ow!" she cried.

Mom tried to comfort Kelly, but Kelly kept crying. "I'll give you a piggyback ride," Mom said. She handed the picnic basket to Jason.

Kelly stopped crying and gave her book to Jason.

Jason reluctantly took the basket and the book. He said, "She's not really hurt, she's just being a pest."

"Jason!" Mom warned.

As he walked, the picnic basket bumped against his leg. "I wish I were at home sketching," he thought.

"Come on, we're almost at the park," Mom said. Jason saw that his mom was upset, so he tried to summon a smile.

That made his mom feel better. She said, "I made your favorite lunch. We have ham sandwiches, lemonade, and watermelon."

Jason said, "Thanks, Mom. They are my favorites."

STOP AND CHECK

How does Jason feel about his sister?

Chapter 2 | The Sting

Jason felt better when they got to the park. He lay down on the blanket and <u>munched</u> on a sandwich. He looked up at the vastness of the blue summer sky.

Suddenly, his mom recoiled. "Ouch! I think I've been stung," she exclaimed.

Jason and Kelly sat down next to Mom and examined her foot. She said, "I think it's a bee sting."

Jason looked at the tiny red bump on Mom's foot and asked, "Do you want me to pull out the stinger?"

"It's okay," Mom said. She flicked away the stinger with her fingernail. "It really hurts, though."

"Are you *really* okay, Mom?" Jason asked.

"I'm fine. I just need to rest for a minute. Could you take Kelly to the swings?"

Language Detective	<u>Munched</u> is a past tense verb. Find other past tense verbs on this page.

"I want Mom to push me," Kelly complained.

"Go with Jason. I'll come after I put some cold water on the bee sting," Mom said.

Jason roused himself and took Kelly's hand. "Come on, pest. Mom needs some peace and quiet."

Kelly agreed. "All right, but come really soon, okay, Mom?"

"You're very persistent today," Mom laughed.

Jason pushed Kelly on the swing, but she complained about everything. She said that Jason was pushing her too slowly, then not high enough. He couldn't do anything right.

"Stop complaining!" Jason shouted.

"I want Mom to do it. I want Mom!" she cried.

"Stop being so selfish," Jason said. He pushed her sideways, and Kelly complained to Mom.

lemonade

blanket

watermelon

Mom was splashing cold water on her foot. Jason could see that she was in pain.

Jason walked over to his mom.

"Are you being nice to your sister?" she asked him.

"No," he responded. Jason looked down at the grass. He didn't want to look at his mom's face. Then he noticed her foot. "Mom, that looks terrible."

His mom's foot was inflamed and swollen.

"It's getting worse," she said.

Jason said, "My friend Eduardo is allergic to bee stings. Maybe you're allergic to bee stings, too."

Mom responded, "Maybe, but I've never had a reaction like this before."

"Eduardo has had to go to the emergency room a couple of times. The bee sting could be very serious, Mom. I think we should go home," Jason urged.

Mom said, "I'm sure that I'll feel better soon. I don't want to spoil our day." She started to hobble toward Kelly.

STOP AND CHECK

Why was Jason worried about his mom's foot?

Chapter 3 | A Severe Reaction

Jason had a real dilemma. His mom was pretending that she was okay because she didn't want Kelly to be worried. But Jason knew that allergic reactions could be dangerous. He really wanted his mom to go home. He saw Kelly's book, and he had an idea.

"Hey, Kelly, can you ride piggyback and read your book at the same time?" he asked.

"Yes I can because I'm a great reader," Kelly responded.

"Jump on my back and show me. Mom, let's go," he said. Mom agreed.

"Guess what, Kelly? I can gallop like a horse," Jason said.

"Okay, then, giddyup," Kelly laughed.

"You go on ahead. I'll walk behind you," Mom said.

Jason lifted his sister onto his back. He held the book with one hand so she could read. Then he said, "Read your book." Kelly read the book aloud. It was hard for Jason, but he didn't complain. "That's excellent reading, Kelly," he said.

path

bench

9

Jason took off at a fast gallop, then he turned back to check on Mom. He stopped suddenly, and Kelly began to cry.

Mom's face was swollen and red. She was swaying as she limped along. Jason was scared, but he knew that he had to stay calm.

"You should sit down," he told Mom. "You could be having a really bad allergic reaction. Eduardo called it anaphylactic shock." Jason put Kelly on a park bench. Then he helped his mom sit down next to Kelly.

"Are you feeling okay?" asked Jason.

"I can't breathe very well," Mom said feebly.

"Eduardo says that it's good to stay calm, so you need to sit still."

Mom stood up. "I think I'm okay now. I just need to get home, put some ice on my foot, and take a pill for the swelling."

Jason had to think fast about what he should do.

In Other Words left quickly. En español, *took off* quiere decir *salio muy rápido*.

Then he remembered what Eduardo had told him. He'd said that he felt confused when he had an allergic reaction. Maybe his mother was confused, too.

"I think you should stop walking. Your foot has swollen up more, probably from walking," Jason cautioned her.

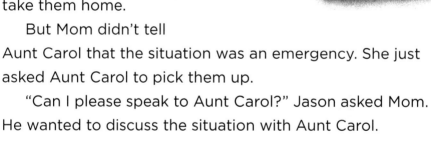

cell phone

Mom took out her cell phone and called Aunt Carol. She wanted to find out if Aunt Carol could take them home.

But Mom didn't tell Aunt Carol that the situation was an emergency. She just asked Aunt Carol to pick them up.

"Can I please speak to Aunt Carol?" Jason asked Mom. He wanted to discuss the situation with Aunt Carol.

STOP AND CHECK

How did Jason get his mom and sister to agree to go home?

Chapter 4 | Emergency Call

Mom handed the phone to Jason, and he moved away from the bench. "I think Mom's having a severe allergic reaction," he whispered to Aunt Carol.

Aunt Carol asked, "How bad is it?"

"It's serious. Her face and foot are swollen. I want to call an ambulance. She seems confused, and she isn't breathing very well," Jason said.

His aunt told him, "It sounds like an emergency. Call an ambulance, and I'll meet you at the hospital."

Jason hung up, then dialed 911. He asked for an ambulance and told the operator their location. The operator asked to speak to his mom. "But she doesn't know I've called you," he said.

"You need to tell her," the operator advised.

ambulance

Jason walked back to the bench. "Mom, I've called an ambulance, and you need to talk to the operator." He passed the phone to his mom.

Mom answered the operator's questions. Jason noticed that his mom's voice sounded weak.

At last they heard a siren.

"Is that the ambulance?" Kelly asked.

"I hope so," Jason responded.

Mom squeezed his hand. "I do, too," she whispered. "It was a good idea to call them, Jason."

"You'll be okay. They're here now," he reassured her. He and Kelly jumped up and waved at the ambulance.

Language Detective	Hope is a present tense verb. Find another present tense verb on this page.

The paramedics checked Mom's pulse. Then they placed an oxygen mask over her mouth so she could breathe more comfortably.

"I didn't know I was allergic. I feel so foolish," Mom mumbled through the oxygen mask.

One of the paramedics helped her onto a stretcher. She said, "It's fortunate that your son knew about allergic reactions. And you're lucky he called us quickly."

They wheeled Mom toward the ambulance and gave her an injection.

"We'll take you to the hospital and monitor you for a while. It's best to be careful," the other paramedic added.

"What about the children?" Mom asked.

"They can come with us in the ambulance."

"Will you play the sirens?" Kelly asked.

Jason said, "Shhhh, Kelly!"

"It's okay," said the paramedic. "But we won't need the siren because your mom is going to be fine."

Jason and Kelly rode in the back of the ambulance. Mom lay on the stretcher.

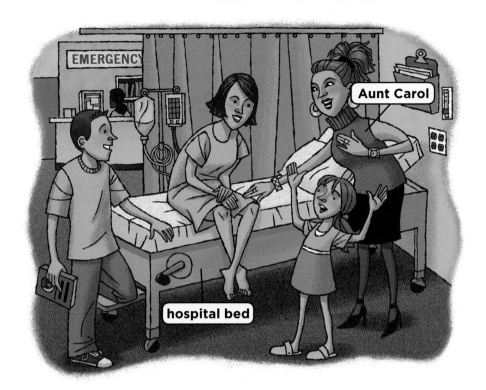

Aunt Carol

hospital bed

Kelly asked questions about the paramedics' equipment. Suddenly Jason felt very tired, and he closed his eyes. He let the paramedics answer Kelly's questions.

Aunt Carol was at the hospital when they arrived. Mom recovered quickly and returned to normal.

Mom said, "You saved my life, Jason." She hugged him tightly. "Sorry I ruined our day in the park."

"Are you joking?" Kelly squeaked. "It was the best day ever! When will you call the ambulance again, Jason?"

Jason rolled his eyes. "Not for a really long time I hope," he laughed.

STOP AND CHECK

How did Jason get his mom to the hospital?

Summarize

Use important details from *Think Hard, Think Fast* to summarize how Jason changed by facing challenges. Use the graphic organizer to help you.

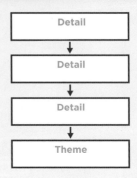

Detail
↓
Detail
↓
Detail
↓
Theme

Text Evidence

1. How do you know that this is realistic fiction? **GENRE**

2. What is the challenge that makes Jason change? **THEME**

3. What does *anaphylactic shock* mean? Read the third paragraph and the surrounding paragraphs on page 10 to find clues about its meaning. **PARAGRAPH CLUES**

4. Use details from the story to write about how Jason's actions support the author's message. **WRITE ABOUT READING**

Compare Texts
Read about a family that has to meet an
interesting challenge.

How Many Hands?

Do you know the saying "Many hands make light work"?
Well, my sister and I learned the meaning of it the hard way.

We love to skate. So when Mom took us to the
ice-skating rink, we were excited.

"I bet I'm faster than you," I said to Pippa.

"No, you are not! I'm faster than you," Pippa responded.

"You are too competitive. You always argue about who's
the best," Mom complained.

At the rink, we decided to have a race.

"Let's see who reaches Mom first," I challenged Pippa.
The race began. First, I was ahead, then Pippa was ahead,
then—

BANG! We smashed into Mom.

skate

rink

We had to go to the hospital because I had cracked an elbow and Pippa had sprained her wrist. Mom had hurt her knee very badly.

When we got home, Mom said, "Your ridiculous race caused the accident. Now you have to figure out a way to cooperate with each other."

"What do you mean?" Pippa and I asked together.

Mom said, "I can't move well, so you need to figure out a way to bring in the laundry and make dinner."

It was difficult to take in the laundry using only one hand.

"We have to figure out a way to work together," I said to Pippa.

So Pippa held the clothesline steady while I pulled off the clothespins and took down the laundry. Then we carried the basket together. Mom looked happy when she saw us. We voted to order takeout for dinner.

We quickly found out that many tasks require using two hands. We argued as we tried to take out the trash can. We tried to carry in the groceries, and the bag broke. Then we broke a plate because we were fighting about who should hold the dishes and who should scrub them.

"Stop competing and help each other!" Mom growled. We tried, but being competitive was <u>second nature</u> to us.

At the end of the second day, we were too tired to compete anymore. So we worked together to cook dinner. When it was time to eat, I got a knife, and Pippa got a fork, and we helped each other to cut up our food.

"At last!" Mom said.

Pippa and I have been a great team ever since.

> **In Other Words** part of someone's character. En español, *second nature* quiere decir *algo muy natural*.

plate

Make Connections

How do Pippa and her sister change after their accident? Why do they change? ESSENTIAL QUESTION

In both *Think Hard, Think Fast* and *How Many Hands?*, characters have to work together for a purpose. Compare the ways they do this in each story.
TEXT TO TEXT

Focus on Literary Elements

Simile An author uses a simile to help to describe something. In a simile, an author compares one thing with something else using the words *like* or *as*. For example, to describe how someone ran really fast, the author could say "he ran as fast as the wind." When you are reading, a simile can help you understand better what the author is describing.

Read and Find Here are two examples of similes: "She swam like a dolphin." "Joey was as quiet as a mouse."

Look at page 2 of *Think Hard, Think Fast*. The author writes that Jason's room "looked like a disaster." On page 8, Jason says he can "gallop like a horse."

Your Turn

Work with a partner or in a group. Select one illustration from *Think Hard, Think Fast* or from another story. Describe one person or object in the illustration using similes. Write similes using the words *like* and *as*. Use the sentence frames:

___ like ___.

___ as ___ as ___.

Present the illustration and similes to the class.